MAKE WAY FOR WINGED EROS

A Book of Days

WOMEN
ON SEXUAL LIBERATION
AND LOVE

CONCEPT AND TEXT BY JACKIE RICE

POMEGRANATE ARTBOOKS

SAN FRANCISCO

Published by Pomegranate Artbooks
Box 6099, Rohnert Park, CA 94927

© 1993 Jackie Rice

ISBN 1-56640-446-0

Designed by Bonnie Smetts Design

Printed in Hong Kong

FIRST EDITION

LINKING EROTICISM TO EMOTION, TO LOVE, TO A
SELECTION OF A CERTAIN PERSON, PERSONALIZING,
INDIVIDUALIZING, THAT WILL BE THE WORK OF WOMEN.

—Anaïs Nin

January

George Sand

FRENCH, 1804–1876

George Sand was one of the most talked about figures and most widely read authors of her time. She was the prototype of the modern woman who lived an independent life and believed that all women were entitled to sexual freedom. George was famed for her scandalous affairs, most notably her liaison with the composer Chopin, and for her masculine attire and pleasures, such as smoking cigars. She advocated the social and sexual equality of women and condemned the subordination of women within the institution of marriage. Her autobiographical novel *Lelia* (1833), the story of a woman incapable of finding physical or emotional satisfaction in her relationships with men, brought her international fame. She wrote some eighty novels in all.

1

2

Intimacy without love is a

loathsome thing to consider.

—George Sand
in Histoire de ma vie

MON

Re-entry workshop
1-5 PM
Classroom Unit 1
lecture hall

3

9:15 Alex

TUES

STEVENSON ORIENTATION
9:00 AM RM 150

4

Where love is absent there

can be no woman.

—*George Sand*

in Lelia

PSYCH DEPT ORIENTATION WED
1:00-2:00 THIMAN 3

5

Search as I may for the remedies to

sore injustice, endless misery and

the incurable passions which trouble

the union of the sexes, I can see no

remedy but the power of breaking

and reforming the marriage bond.

—*George Sand*

in Letters of George Sand

FIRST DAY OF CLASSES!   THURS

6

7

8

9

10

FIRST FIG

My candle burns at both ends;

It will not last the night;

But, ah, my foes, and oh, my friends—

It gives a lovely light!

—*Edna St. Vincent Millay*
in A Few Figs from Thistles

III

Oh, think not I am faithful to a vow!
Faithless am I save to love's self alone.
Were you not lovely I would leave you now:
After the feet of beauty fly my own.
Were you not still my hunger's rarest food,
And water ever to my wildest thirst,
I would desert you—think not but I would!—
And seek another as I sought you first.
But you are mobile as the veering air,
And all your charms more changeful than the tide,
Wherefore to be inconstant is no care:
I have but to continue at your side.
So wanton, light and false, my love, are you,
I am most faithless when I most am true.

—*Edna St. Vincent Millay*
in A Few Figs from Thistles

Edna St. Vincent Millay

AMERICAN, 1892–1950

When Edna St. Vincent Millay was twenty-six she moved to Greenwich Village to live among other struggling writers and artists. There she began writing poetry that reflected her belief in the independent woman and expressed her unconventional view of love as ephemeral. Edna did not believe in compromising her intellectual freedom for love. There were, however, two men who had a lasting influence on her: poet Arthur Ficke, with whom she had an affair, and Eugen Boissevain, whom she married in 1923. Edna immortalized the love she and Ficke shared in *Second April* (1921), the most lyrical of her love sonnets. With the publication of her drama *Aria de Capo* (1919, published 1921) and her impudent love sonnets in *A Few Figs from Thistles* (1920), she became enormously popular. Edna was awarded the Pulitzer Prize for *The Harp-Weaver and Other Poems* (1923).

11

12

13

Edna St. Vincent Millay, c. 1923. Photograph by Eugen Boissevain. Courtesy Vassar College Library.

Victoria Woodhull

AMERICAN, 1838–1927

Victoria Claflin Woodhull distinguished herself from other suffragists of her period by advocating "free love" and drawing a connection between feminism and sexual freedom. She believed in a single standard of morality for both women and men and spoke out against the victimization of prostitutes. Victoria and her sister Tennessee published a weekly radical newspaper that discussed such issues as birth control, abortion, venereal disease and sexual liberation. With the support of railroad tycoon Cornelius Vanderbilt, they also established a successful stock brokerage. In 1872, at a time when women did not yet have the right to vote, Victoria was nominated for the U.S. presidency by the Equal Rights party, with Frederick Douglass as her running mate. In 1877 the sisters moved to England, where Victoria entered her third marriage and Tennessee her second. Both women eventually became well-known philanthropists.

Re-entry Open House
7:30 - 9:30 Cornell Broadcast House

14

15

16

The wife who submits to sexual intercourse against her wishes or desires virtually commits suicide; while the husband who compels it commits murder.

—Victoria Woodhull
in Elixir of Life *speech*

17

18

I have an inalienable, constitutional and natural right to love whom I may, to love as long or as short a period as I can, to change that love every day if I please.

—Victoria Woodhull
in Woodhull and Claflin's
Weekly, *1871*

19

20

Marie Stopes

ENGLISH, 1880–1958

Marie Stopes was a brilliant scholar
and distinguished scientist. She
received her Ph.D. degree in 1904
and subsequently lectured on paleo-
botany at the University of London
and at Manchester University, where
she was the first woman member of
the science faculty. Her first marriage was annulled after five years
on the grounds that it was never
consummated. In response to her
sexually unfulfilled marriage, Marie
wrote and published *Married Love*
and *Wise Parenthood* in 1918. The
books defended the married
woman's right to reciprocal sexual
enjoyment and her right to control
her reproduction. Marie committed
her life to awakening the sexual consciousness of married couples. With
her second husband, Humphrey
Verdon Roe, she founded the first
birth control clinic in Britain.

21

22

From *Passionate Crusaders: The Life of Marie Stopes*, © 1977 by Ruth Hall. Reproduced by
permission of Harcourt Brace Jovanovich, Inc.

We have studied the wave-
lengths of water, of sound,
of light; but when will the
sons and daughters of men
study the sex-tide in woman
and learn the laws of her
Periodicity of Recurrence of
desire?

       —Marie Stopes
       in Married Love

23

24

25

Each heart knows instinctively that
it is only a mate who can give full
comprehension of all the potential
greatness of the soul, and have tender laughter for all the childlike
wonder that lingers so enchantingly
even in the whitehaired.

       —Marie Stopes
       in Married Love

26

27

28

29

> Why are women...so much
> more interesting to men
> than men are to women?
>
> —*Virginia Woolf*
> *in* A Room of One's Own

30

31

> I do not believe the woman exists
> who would have the courage to have
> lived it as I have done.
>
> —*Josephine Baker*
> *in a press interview,*
> *Music Center, Los Angeles,*
> *September 20, 1973*

IT MATTERS ALL
A little more or less of health?
    What does it matter!
A little more or less of wealth?
    A boon to scatter!
But more or less of love your own to call,
    It matters all!

—*Kate Chopin*

February

Romaine Brooks

AMERICAN, 1874–1970

Born to a wealthy but mentally
unstable mother, Romaine Brooks
experienced an unhappy and trau-
matic childhood. At age twenty-one
she escaped to Rome, where she
studied art. Later she lived on the
island of Capri, where she shared a
studio with other homosexual
artists. After moving to Paris, she
became known for her lesbian portraits and paintings of androgynous
nudes, described as "icily erotic."
Romaine is also remembered for her
relationship with Natalie Barney,
which lasted over forty years.

1

From *The Amazon of Letters* by George Wickes. Courtesy George Wickes.

2

Why blame the cause of past tribula-

tions if their effect in the present

stands for strength and individuality?

—*Romaine Brooks*
in No Pleasant Memories

3

4

Society considers the sex experiences
of a man as attributes of his general
development, while similar experiences in the life of a woman are
looked upon as a terrible calamity, a
loss of honor and of all that is good
and noble in the human being.

—Emma Goldman
in The Hypocrisy of Puritanism

5

6

7

8

She had not yet learnt that the
loneliest place in this world is
the no-man's-land of sex.

—Radclyffe Hall
in The Well of Loneliness

9

FEBRUARY

10

11

12

13

14

To love him genuinely is to love him in his otherness and in that freedom by which he escapes. One renounces being in order that there may be that being which one is not.... No existence can be validly fulfilled if it is limited to itself.

—*Simone de Beauvoir*
in Ethics of Ambiguity

Love is not a sentiment worthy of respect.

—*Colette*

15

Trembling was all living,
living was all loving, some
one was then the other one.

—*Gertrude Stein*
in Ada

16

17

Romaine Brooks. *Le Trajet* [The Journey] (detail), c. 1900. Oil on canvas, 45⅝ x 75¼ in.
National Museum of American Art, Smithsonian Institution. Gift of the artist 1968.18.3

I was trademarked as a vampire.
Being a woman in the profession of
acting, I played my part. Being a
woman who respects her art, who
really believes that acting is the
highest form of feminine expression,
I did not confuse my own identity
with the parts I played.

—*Theda Bara*
in "How I Became a Film Vampire,"
Forum, *June/July 1919*

18

19

Romaine Brooks. *Chasseresse* [Huntress], 1920. Oil on canvas, 51¾ x 38¼ in. National
Museum of American Art, Smithsonian Institution. Gift of the artist .

The best lovers I ever had
were homosexuals.

—Louise Brooks
in a letter
to Kevin Brownlow,
October 25, 1969

20

21

22

To attempt to raise ourselves above
human beings is ridiculous; we cannot extirpate our passions, nor is it
necessary that we should, though it
may be wise sometimes not to stray
too near a precipice, lest we fall over
before we are aware.

—Mary Wollstonecraft
in "Love," from Thoughts on the
Education of Daughters

23

24

And if I loved you Wednesday,
Well, what is that to you?
I do not love you Thursday—
So much is true.

And why you come complaining
Is more than I can see.
I loved you Wednesday,—yes—but what
Is that to me?

—*Edna St. Vincent Millay*
in A Few Figs from Thistles

My life has known but two motives—
Love and Art—often Love destroyed
Art, and often the imperious call of
Art put a tragic end to Love. For
these two have no accord but only
constant battle.

—*Isadora Duncan*

25

26

27

As long as we continue to see, to
feel only in another, all nature to
us is under different forms, the
spring, the prospect and the cli-
mate, which we have enjoyed with
the beloved object.

—*Germaine de Staël*
in Influence of Passion

28

29

Marriage is as certain a bane
to love as lending is to
friendship; I'll neither ask
nor give a vow.

—*Aphra Behn*

Romaine Brooks. *Ida Rubenstein,* 1917. Oil on canvas, 46¾ x 37 in. National Museum of
American Art, Smithsonian Institution/Art Resource, New York. Gift of the artist 1968.18.10.

March

Elizabeth Barrett Browning

ENGLISH, 1806–1861

Elizabeth Barrett Browning was an emancipated writer who emphasized the female voice and wrote some of the finest English love poems of her time. A sickly child, she spent much of her early life housebound, reading voraciously and writing poetry. In 1844 she published *Poems,* which brought her public acclaim and prompted a correspondence with poet Robert Browning. Elizabeth and Robert's relationship developed into a courtship—kept secret from her tyrannical father. In 1846 the couple married and moved to Italy, where Elizabeth wrote her famous *Sonnets from the Portuguese* (1850), proclaiming her love for Robert. In opposition to the sexual decorum of the time, Elizabeth wrote her love sonnets from a woman's point of view, proclaiming her "right" to love rather than being merely the object of love. Her most popular novel in verse, *Aurora Leigh* (1857), condemns the double standard of Victorian morality.

1

2

XI

Thus, if thou wilt prove me, Dear,

Woman's love no fable,

I will love thee—half a year—

As a man is able.

—*Elizabeth Barrett Browning*
in "A Man's Requirements"

3

4

XLIII

How do I love thee? Let me count the ways.

I love thee to the depth and breadth and height

My soul can reach, when feeling out of sight

For the ends of Being and ideal Grace.

I love thee to the level of everyday's

Most quiet need, by sun and candle-light.

I love thee freely, as men strive for Right;

I love thee purely, as they turn from Praise.

I love thee with the passion put to use

Oh—I hold to my rights,

though you overcome me in

In my old griefs, and with my childhood's faith.

most other things. And it is

I love thee with a love I seemed to lose

my right to love you better

With my lost saints,—I love thee with the breath,

than I could do if I were more

Smiles, tears, of all my life!—and if God choose,

worthy to be loved by you.

I shall but love thee better after death.

—*Elizabeth Barrett Browning*

in Sonnets from the Portuguese

—*Elizabeth Barrett Browning*
in a letter to Robert Browning

5

6

7

8

9

A woman has no other choice than to be unfaithful or to be only half herself. In her love she is like a tree awaiting the lightning which will sunder it, but also like the tree, she desires to put forth an abundance of blooms.

—*Lou Andreas-Salomé*

Erotic life as a whole contains all of sexuality symbolically in itself, so that physical union is an absolute symbol of spiritual union, particularly in the case of woman, who unites opposites more completely in her own more integrated being.

—*Lou Andreas-Salomé*
in The Freud Journal

Lou Andreas-Salomé

GERMAN, 1861–1937

At age twenty Lou Andreas-Salomé left Russia for Germany, where she met and became intimately associated with a number of men. Among them were such notables as Friedrich Wilhelm Nietzsche, who proposed to her but was refused; Rainer Rilke, who immortalized his love for her in his poems; and Sigmund Freud, with whom she had a close mentor relationship. Lou was convinced that women were happier than and superior to men and described femaleness as essentially "self-sufficient." Striving toward self-realization, she fought propriety and convention and lived her life free of subordination. At fifty she became one of the few female practitioners of psychoanalysis, which she pursued for the next twenty-five years. A celebrated thinker and writer, she wrote *Erotic Thoughts on the Problem of Love* and *The Freud Journal,* among other publications.

10

11

Kate Chopin

AMERICAN, 1851–1904

Kate Chopin did not begin to write until age thirty. Widowed and responsible for six children, she first wrote tales for children and then several volumes of short stories and anecdotes depicting Creole and Cajun life in Louisiana, most notably *Bayou Folk* (1894) and *A Night in Acadie* (1897). Kate is best known, however, for her novel *The Awakening* (1899), which was boycotted for its frank message of women's quest for sexual fulfillment and independence. The book portrayed a woman's rejection of the constraints of marriage and motherhood in pursuit of her sexual and creative freedom. It received such harsh criticism that Kate never published again.

12

13

By all the codes which I am
acquainted with, I am a devilishly
wicked specimen of the sex. But
some way I can't convince myself
that I am.

—*Kate Chopin*
in The Awakening

14

15

16

I give myself where I choose.

—*Kate Chopin*
in The Awakening

17

18

19

20

The most beautiful life is the one spent in creating one-self, not in procreating.

—*Natalie Barney*

21

22

There are only two possibilities in life: to be someone or to be preoccupied with someone. One demands great intelligence, the other, a big heart. Within these alternatives, life is a discouraging voyage from one ocean to another.

—*Natalie Barney*

23

Natalie Barney

AMERICAN, 1876–1972

Natalie Barney, the "Amazon of Paris," was one of the most famous Americans in Paris in the 1920s. Muse to a number of writers, she was infamous for her seductive powers of mind and body. Natalie believed that love was fleeting but true friendship was eternal. She had sapphic romances with Liane de Pougy, the queen of demimonde; poet Vivien Renee; Dolly Wilde; and painter Romaine Brooks, with whom she shared more than forty years of her life. A legend in her own time, Natalie was renowned for her emancipated ideas, her avowal of lesbianism and her literary salon, the "Temple of Friendship."

24

25

26

From *The Amazon of Letters*, by George Wickes. Courtesy George Wickes .

27

28

29

30

31

A mutual and satisfied sexual act is of great benefit to the average woman; the magnetism of it is health giving and acts as a beautifier and tonic. When it is not desired on the part of the woman and she has no response, it should not take place. This is an act of prostitution and is degrading to the woman's finer sensibility, all the marriage certificates on earth to the contrary notwithstanding.

—*Margaret Sanger*
in Family Limitations

The problem of birth control has arisen directly from the effort of the feminine spirit to free itself from bondage.

—*Margaret Sanger*
in Woman and the New Race

April

Margaret Sanger

AMERICAN, 1879–1966

Personal experience as one of eleven children and her work as a public health nurse helped turn Margaret Sanger into a pioneer of the birth control movement in the United States. Alarmed by the infant mortality rate and the number and dire consequences of self-induced abortions among poor women, Margaret crusaded for the dissemination of contraceptive information and devices. In 1914 she began publishing a monthly paper called *The Woman Rebel*, which advocated birth control. But the paper was deemed "obscene" under the Comstock Act of 1873, and the post office refused to mail it. Margaret also secretly printed a pamphlet called *Family Limitations*, which provided explicit information on contraceptives. She was indicted in 1915 for sending birth control information through the mail and arrested in 1916 for conducting a birth control clinic in Brooklyn, New York. Eventually, however, she gained public support and was able to open a legal birth control clinic in New York City (1923), which operated until the 1970s. Throughout her life she continued to sponsor conferences, and she lectured and helped establish clinics in many countries in Europe, Asia and Africa. She also wrote several books, including *Woman and the New Race* (1920), *Happiness in Marriage* (1926) and an autobiography (1938).

1

2

Alice Neel

AMERICAN, 1900–1984

Alice Neel lived the bohemian artistic life-style of the 1930s, residing first in Greenwich Village and later in Spanish Harlem. Perhaps due in part to her own emotional breakdown and financial strife, her paintings provide sensitive and honest insight into the emotional suffering and human deprivation of her models. Alice is best known for her feminist portraits of women and children, her unconventional nudes and her candid depictions of pregnancy and motherhood. In the 1960s and '70s she enjoyed public recognition for her portraits of New York art figures.

3

4

This is the rebellion of the women of our age of transition, who have not yet learned how to harmonize inner freedom and independence with the all-consuming passion of love.

—*Alexandra Kollontai*
in Autobiography of a Sexually
Emancipated Woman

5

6

7

If the world is ever to give
birth to true companionship
and oneness, not marriage,
but love will be the parent.

—*Emma Goldman*
in Marriage and Love

8

9

10

11

12

13

14

15

Love is woman's virtue; it is for love that she glories in her sins, it is from love that she acquires the heroism to defy her remorse. The more dearly it costs her to commit the crime, the more she will have deserved at the hands of the man she loves. It is like the fanaticism that places the dagger in the hand of the religious enthusiast.

—George Sand
in Indiana

I am seeking the truth about sexual intercourse, and I will follow it if it leads me either to heaven or hell.

—Victoria Woodhull
in The Scarecrows of Sexual
Freedom *speech*

16

No matter what the rules are, when

one is painting, one creates one's

own world.

—Alice Neel
in a doctoral address,
Moore College of Art,
June 1, 1971

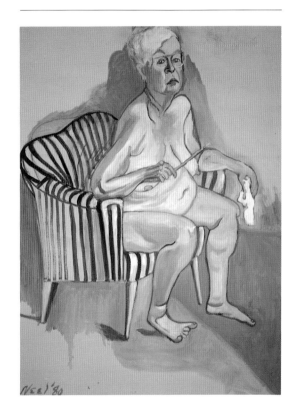

17

Alice Neel. *Self-Portrait*, 1980. Oil on canvas, 54 x 40 in. Collection: National Portrait
Gallery, Washington, D.C. Courtesy Robert Miller Gallery, New York.

18

19

Without passion, love would be a flaccid, lifeless thing. Passion is the driving power of life. It cannot be denied, destroyed or thrust aside. It must and it will find expression in some way—in destruction if its power be denied or not directed to creative ends. While it is a cruel master, it is also a willing slave.

—*Margaret Sanger*
in Happiness in Marriage

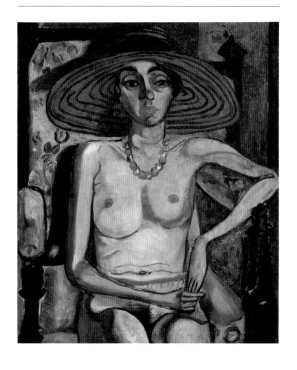

Alice Neel. *Rhoda Meyers with Blue Hat,* 1930. Oil on canvas, 27½ x 23¼ in. Robert Miller Gallery, New York.

By God, I have never understood why people who are in
love in a predominantly sensual way get married.

—Lou Andreas-Salomé

20

21

22

Each couple, after marriage, must
study themselves, and the lover and
the beloved must do what best serves
them both and gives them the highest degree of mutual joy and power.

—Marie Stopes
in Married Love

23

24

|

Love me Sweet, with all thou art,
Feeling, thinking, seeing;
Love me in the lightest part,
Love me in full being.

*—Elizabeth Barrett Browning
in "A Man's Requirements"*

25

In blaming indiscretion, it
seems that we forget the good
things that derive from it.

—Natalie Barney

26

27

Sex expression, rightly understood,
is the consummation of love, its
completion and its consecration.

*—Margaret Sanger
in* Happiness in Marriage

28

The right to vote, or equal civil rights, may be good demands, but true emancipation begins neither at the polls nor in courts. It begins in woman's soul.

—*Emma Goldman*
in Tragedy of Women's
Emancipation

29

30

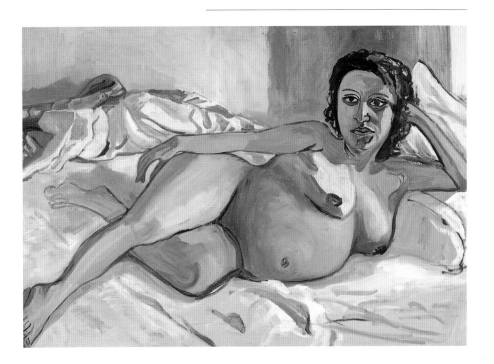

May

Frida Kahlo

MEXICAN, 1910–1954

At age eighteen Frida Kahlo was in a
bus accident that crushed her pelvis
and spine and left her temporarily
bedridden and permanently in pain.
While convalescing she began to
paint and became infatuated with
the famous muralist Diego Rivera,
whom she married in 1929. Frida's
paintings, most notably her self-
portraits, reflect the intensity of her
physical and emotional pain, which
was compounded by a series of
unsuccessful operations, her inabil-
ity to bear children and her stormy
relationship with Rivera. Admired
for her art, she was also noted for
her sensual personality, exotic style
of dress and commitment to "Viva la
Vida"—live the life.

1

2

Man is a human being with sexuality;
woman is a complete individual,
equal to the male, only if she, too, is
a human being with sexuality. To
renounce her femininity is to
renounce a part of her humanity.

—Simone de Beauvoir
in The Second Sex

3

4

5

It [Theda Bara] is a name, therefore, that stands for some emotional
value in a world where romance is a
food that all hearts crave.

—Theda Bara
in "How I Became a Film Vampire,"
Forum, *June/July 1919*

6

7

8

9

If you have a body in which you are born to a certain amount of pain...why should you not, when the occasion presents, draw from this same body the maximum of pleasure?

—*Isadora Duncan*
in My Life

Feet—what do I need them for, if I have wings to fly?

—*Frida Kahlo*
in her diary

Frida Kahlo. *Self-Portrait with Cropped Hair*, 1940. Oil on canvas, 15¾ x 11 in. Collection, The Museum of Modern Art, New York. Gift of Edgar Kaufmann, Jr. Photograph © 1992 The Museum of Modern Art, New York.

10

11

Love, unsupported by esteem, must soon expire, or lead to depravity; as, on the contrary, when a worthy person is the object, it is the greatest incentive to improvement, and has the best effect on the manners and temper.

—*Mary Wollstonecraft*
in "Love," from Thoughts on the
Education of Daughters

12

But do not confuse sex performance with "love." Contrary to all this stuff women are putting out today about the need for having orgasms, sexual satisfaction never holds people together.

—*Louise Brooks*
in a letter

13

14

15

16

Love ceases to be a pleasure
when it ceases to be a secret.

—*Aphra Behn*

Frida Kahlo. *Two Nudes in the Jungle,* 1939. Oil on sheet metal, 9⅞ x 11⅞ in. Courtesy Mary-
Anne Martin.

Love is the sole passion of
women.

—*Germaine de Staël*
in Influence of Passion

17

18

Is the contemporary person psycho-
logically able to cope with "free
love"? What about the jealousy that
eats into even the best human souls?
And that deeply rooted sense of
property that demands the possession not only of the body but also of
the soul of another?... And the bitter
and desperate feeling of desertion, of
limitless loneliness, which is experienced when the loved ceases to love
and leaves? Where can the lonely
person, who is an individualist to the
very core of his being, find solace?

—*Alexandra Kollontai*
in The Social Basis
of the Woman Question

19

20

21

22

23

24

25

26

What we will have to reach, the ideal, is the recognition of woman's sensual nature, the acceptance of its needs, the knowledge of the variety of temperaments, and the joyous attitude towards it as a part of nature, as natural as the growth of a flower, the tides, the movements of planets.

—*Anaïs Nin*
in Cities of the Interior

I felt that one could both love another, to the point of submitting to him, and love oneself, to the point of hating him who subjugates us.

—*George Sand*
in Lelia

27

28

To woman, by nature, belongs the
right of sexual determination. When
the instinct is aroused in her, then
and then only should commerce follow. When woman rises from sexual
slavery into freedom…and man is
obliged to respect this freedom, then
will this instinct become pure and
holy; then will woman be raised from
the iniquity and morbidness in which
she now wallows for existence.

—*Victoria Woodhull*
in Tried as by Fire

Frida Kahlo. *Self-Portrait with Thorn Necklace and Hummingbird,* 1940. Oil on canvas, 25 x
20 in. The Harry Ransom Humanities Research Center Art Collection, The University of
Texas at Austin. Reproduction authorized by Instituto Nacional de Bellas Artes y Literatura.

29

Women have served all these
centuries as looking-glasses
possessing the magic and
delicious power of reflecting
the figure of man at twice its
natural size.

—*Virginia Woolf*
in A Room of One's Own

30

31

I began life with a tremendous,
absurd ideal of marriage; then my
bird's eye view of many marriages
disgusted me, and I thought I must
be asking what was not to be had.
But that has passed, too. Now I only
ask for someone to make me vehe-
ment, and then I'll marry them.

—*Virginia Woolf*
in a letter to Lytton Strachey

|
Love, though for this you riddle me with darts,
And drag me at your chariot till I die,—
Oh, heavy prince! Oh, panderer of hearts!—
Yet hear me tell how in their throats they lie
Who shout you mighty: thick about my hair,
Day in, day out, your ominous arrows purr,
Who still am free, unto no querulous care
A fool, and in no temple worshiper!
I, that have bared me to your quiver's fire,
Lifted my face into its puny rain,
Do wreathe you Impotent to Evoke Desire
As you are Powerless to Elicit Pain!
(Now will the god, for blasphemy so brave,
Punish me, surely, with the shaft I crave!)

—*Edna St. Vincent Millay*
in A Few Figs from Thistles

June

Virginia Woolf

ENGLISH, 1882–1941

Virginia Woolf, a prolific novelist and essayist, was well known for her innovativeness and her poetic, symbolic, visual prose. In her novels she emphasized the consciousness of her characters over plot and characterization, moving from mind to mind throughout each book. Perhaps most notable among her feminist novels is *A Room of One's Own* (1929), in which she explored the female writer's need for privacy, financial independence and an "androgynous mind." She also examined women's rights in *Three Guineas* (1928).

Virginia married Leonard Woolf, a critic and writer on economics, in 1912, and the couple became cornerstones of the Bloomsbury Group, whose meetings were often held at the Woolfs' home. Virginia dedicated her novel *Orlando* (1928) to Vita Sackville-West, a member of the group with whom she had a romantic relationship. Having already experienced two mental breakdowns, in 1895 and 1915, Virginia drowned herself in 1941 because she feared the onset of another breakdown from which she might not recover.

1

2

JUNE

3

4

It is exactly because pure
and prosperous women
choose to ignore vice, that
miserable women suffer
wrong by it everywhere.

—*Elizabeth Barrett*
Browning

5

6

If cold marble so stirs us, how much
more the warmth and vitality of living beauty! Any well-formed young
man or woman is immeasurably more
graceful when free from the clinging
follies of modern dress, while a beautiful woman's body has a supernal
loveliness at which no words short of
a poetic rapture can even hint.

—*Marie Stopes*
in Married Love

7

Paula Modersohn-Becker

GERMAN, 1876–1907

Paula Modersohn-Becker's unconventional paintings were misunderstood in her time but were a precursor to modernist art. Passionately devoted to her painting, in her early twenties Paula joined an artists' colony outside Worpswede and began painting peasants and children from the village. She made numerous trips to Paris, where she was influenced by the postimpressionist movement. She is best remembered for her primitive images of pregnant women and sensual nudes surrounded by symbols of fertility, including a self-portrait, pregnant at age thirty, on her fifth wedding anniversary. She died less than one month after delivery.

8

9

From *Paula Modersohn-Becker*, 1985. Courtesy Verlag Atelier im Bauernhaus.

10

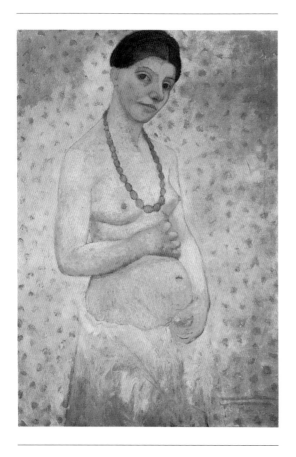

My experience is that happiness does not increase in marriage. Marriage removes the illusion, deeply embedded previously, that somewhere there is a soul-mate.

—from Paula Modersohn-Becker's diary, Easter Sunday, 1902

11

Only when there is a twofold alter-
nation between masculinity and
femininity can two persons be more
than one, no longer regarding each
other merely as a goal (like miserable halves which need to be stuck
together to form a whole) but rather
committed together to a goal outside themselves. Only then are love
and creation, natural fulfillment
and cultural activity, no longer
opposites, but one.

—Lou Andreas-Salomé

12

13

14

What could love, the unsolved
mystery, count for in the face
of this possession of self-
assertion which she suddenly
recognized as the strongest
impulse of her being?

—Kate Chopin
in The Story of an Hour

15

16

17

Those who do not put their
soul in their flesh are
unworthy of life.

—*Natalie Barney*
in Pensees d'une Amazon

18

19

20

Romance, to live, must not be caged
in the atmosphere of tame domestic-
ity, nor deprived of the opportunity
to soar.

—*Margaret Sanger*
in Happiness in Marriage

21

22

Chastity...has, even now, a relative
importance in a woman's life, and
has so wrapped itself round with
nerves and instincts that to cut it

23

free and bring it to the light of day
demands courage of the rarest.

—Virginia Woolf
in To the Lighthouse

Paula Modersohn-Becker. *Self-Portrait,* 1906. Öffentliche Kunstsammlung, Basel.

24

...and you will accord me the sensual satisfaction that is the surcease of love like a sovereign exorcism that will drive out of me the demons of fever, anger, restlessness.

—Colette

25

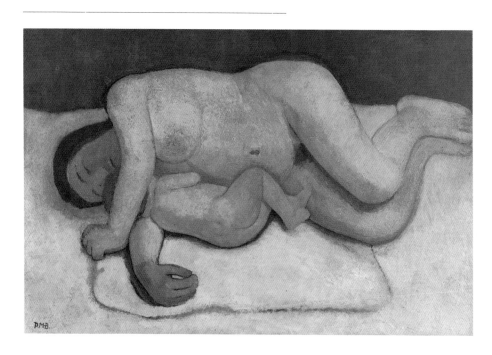

Paula Modersohn-Becker. *Reclining Mother and Child,* 1906. Ludwig Reselius Collection. Böttcherstrasse GMBH, Bremen.

26

If love does not know how to give
and take without restrictions, it is
not love, but a transaction that
never fails to lay stress on a plus and
a minus.

—*Emma Goldman*
in Tragedy of Women's
Emancipation

27

28

29

I'm not immoral, I'm natural.

—*Josephine Baker*

30

July

Josephine Baker

AMERICAN, 1906–1975

Born in St. Louis, Josephine Baker reached young adulthood during the jazz era of the 1920s. She lived and breathed the rich music of the nightclubs and taught herself to sing and dance. Beginning as a chorus girl, she worked her way up to become a lead dancer in American productions. But it was her role as the "Dark Star" of the Follies Bergegre in Paris for which she is best remembered. In one part of the act she appeared topless on a mirror wearing only a short skirt made of rubber bananas. The "Banana Dance" made her an overnight star with a huge public following. Postwar artistic and intellectual circles in France were mesmerized by her exoticism, and she soon became the toast of Paris. Josephine enjoyed a plethora of passionate affairs, was married four times and came to epitomize the spirit of the Jazz Age and the repudiation of Western sexual repression.

1

Art is an elastic sort of love.

—*Josephine Baker*
in Arsenal Pressbook,
September 20, 1933

2

3

4

I dreamed I was floating nude down
a stream on a lily pad and the stream
was lined with thousands of cheering
fans. That might be heaven.

—*Josephine Baker*

5

6

Radclyffe Hall

ENGLISH, 1883–1943

Radclyffe Hall grew up writing poetry, and by her mid twenties she was writing novels. Her most famous novel, *The Well of Loneliness*, was a semi-autobiographical account of homosexual love. Upon its completion in 1928, the London courts ruled the novel obscene and banned its publication in England. During the trial Radclyffe protested, "I have written the life of a woman who is a born invert, and have done so with what I believe to be sincerity and truth; and while I have refused to camouflage in any way, I think I have avoided all unnecessary coarseness."

Radclyffe's first relationship, at age twenty-seven, was with a fifty-year-old woman. Her second involvement, with Una Troubridge, became a lifetime commitment. Only once during this period did Radclyffe become infatuated with a younger woman, Eugenia Souline, to whom she wrote, "My love for you has nothing to do with my devotion to Una."

7

8

9

Acknowledge us, O God,
before the whole world. Give
us also the right to our
existence.

10

—*Radclyffe Hall*
in The Well of Loneliness

11

You're neither unnatural, nor abom-
inable, nor mad; you're as much a
part of what people call nature as
anyone else; only you're unexplained
as yet—you've not got your niche in
creation.

12

—*Radclyffe Hall*
in The Well of Loneliness

13

14

Someday, men and women will rise,
they will reach the mountain peak,
they will meet big and strong and
free, ready to receive, to partake, and
to bask in the golden rays of love.

—Emma Goldman
in Marriage and Love

15

16

17

Love, the strongest and deepest
element in all life, the harbinger of
hope, of joy, of ecstasy; love, the
defier of all laws, of all conventions; love, the freest, the most
powerful molder of human destiny;
how can such an all-compelling
force be synonymous with that poor
little State- and Church-begotten
weed, marriage?

18

—Emma Goldman
in Marriage and Love

Emma Goldman

RUSSIAN AMERICAN, 1869–1940

Emma Goldman was born in a Jewish ghetto in czarist Russia and lived there until age fifteen, when she fled to the United States to escape her tyrannical father. Within a few years she became a leading spokesperson for the anarchist movement in the United States, speaking out on labor rights, opposition to the war, birth control and sexual equality. She was a proponent of free and open relationships between the sexes and felt that the institution of marriage was antithetical to ideal love.

Emma believed that the key to women's emancipation began with their psychological emancipation and that sexual liberation and personal freedom were imperative to self-growth. She was criticized not only by the political right but also by her comrades for her outspokenness on the special oppression of women based solely on their sex. Labeled "Red Emma," she was deported by the United States and later exiled from Russia for her revolutionary ideas.

19

20

Colette

FRENCH, 1873–1954

Colette (Sidonie Gabrielle Colette) penned numerous novels noted for their sensitive, intimate portrayals—particularly of women. Her first success came with her four *Claudine* books (1900–1903), the innocent yet evocative adventures of a young girl and married woman. At age thirty-three she became a music hall dancer and mime while continuing to write. Her most famous book from this period is *La Vagabonde* [The Vagabond] (1911), a story about female self-discovery. In her subsequent masterpiece, *Chéri* (1920), she portrayed women as having traditionally male strengths and sexual desires. In *Les Plaisirs* [The Pleasures], Colette transcended literary taboos and wrote about lesbian love. The thrice-married Colette further defied convention by bobbing her hair, performing onstage semi-nude and living a sexually emancipated life. At age seventy-one she published her last book, the popular *Gigi*, a story of wartime romance. Colette was the first woman president of the Académie Goncourt and the second woman to become a grand officer in the French Legion of Honor.

21

22

23

My true friends have always
given me that supreme proof
of devotion, a spontaneous
aversion for the man I loved.

—*Colette*
in Break of Day

24

25

There are two kinds of love: the love
that is never satisfied and makes you
hateful to everyone, and the love that
is satisfied and turns you into an idiot.

—*Colette*

26

27

28

29

30

31

Some are knowing all of
completely loving being happening and are completely
using that thing completely
using loving being com-
pletely happening.

—*Gertrude Stein*
in A Long Gay Book

Some say alright all but one way of
loving, another says alright all but
another way of loving. . . . I like loving.
I like mostly all the ways any one can
have of having loving feeling in them.
Slowly it has come to be in me that
any way of being a loving one is inter-
esting and not unpleasant to me.

—*Gertrude Stein*
in The Making of Americans

THE PHILOSOPHER

Yet woman's ways are witless ways,
    As any sage will tell,—
And what am I, that I should love
    So wisely and so well?

—*Edna St. Vincent Millay*
in A Few Figs from Thistles

August

Gertrude Stein

AMERICAN, 1874–1946

American expatriate Gertrude Stein lived for most of her adult life in Paris, where she led an artistic and literary salon that included such writers as F. Scott Fitzgerald, Ernest Hemingway and Sherwood Anderson. Passionately interested in modern art, she encouraged and collected the works of Picasso and Matisse, among others. In her own writing she took an innovative approach, emphasizing the sound and rhythm of words over their meanings. Among her books are *Three Lives* (1909), *Tender Buttons* (1914), *The Making of Americans* (1925) and *A Long Gay Book* (1932).

In 1907 Gertrude met Alice B. Toklas and entered a love relationship that would last a lifetime. She wrote about her intimate relationship with Alice in her three-page portrait "Ada" (1941) and in her erotic love poem "Lifting Belly." Stein is probably best known for *The Autobiography of Alice B. Toklas* (1933), an autobiographical work about Stein but presented as her companion's story.

1

2

3

Vanessa Bell

ENGLISH, 1879–1961

Vanessa Bell, the eldest sister of Virginia Woolf, was a painter who had close ties to the Bloomsbury Group, a gathering of writers and intellectuals that centered its activities in Bloomsbury Square in London from 1904 to about 1939. Members of the group included Virginia and Leonard Woolf, Clive Bell, Lytton Strachey, E. M. Forster, Roger Fry, Vita Sackville-West and John Maynard Keynes. In 1906 Vanessa married Clive Bell, but during her marriage she had a passionate affair with Roger Fry, and for almost half a century she had an unconventional companionship with painter Duncan Grant, who was homosexual. In addition to her painting, Vanessa designed textiles, ceramics and woodcuts and illustrated and designed books for her sister Virginia.

4

5

Vanessa Bell, 1930. The Tate Gallery Archives.

6

Lifting belly is so pleased
Lifting belly seeks pleasure.
And she finds it altogether.
Lifting belly is my love.

—*Gertrude Stein*
in "Lifting Belly"

7

8

I realized from the first that I might
meet only one or two human beings
in life I should really like. The rest,
like ships that pass in the night,
mysterious forms, or the crowds that
roll on through streets and streets,
huge waves of a human stream.

—*Theda Bara*
in "How I Became a Film Vampire,"
Forum, *June/July 1919*

9

10

11

12

When I think about you and I begin to try to draw you, but luckily only in the air, I know the shape of all of you pretty well now—even your hands, I think I know almost as well as you know mine. I don't talk about them as much but perhaps I have felt them even more intimately.

—*Vanessa Bell*
in a letter to Roger Fry,
June 23, 1911,
King's College, Cambridge

Vanessa Bell. *Tile design: Spring,* c. 1950. Oil and gouache on paper, 27½ x 27½ in. Anthony d'Offay Gallery, London.

I am a little singular in my thoughts of love and friendship; I must have the first place or none.

—*Mary Wollstonecraft*

13

14

15

We flatter ourselves when we assume that we have restored the sexual integrity which was expurgated by the Victorians.

—*Louise Brooks*

16

17

Love in its present form is a complex

state of mind and body.... [It] is

intricately woven from friendship,

passion, maternal tenderness, infat-

uation, mutual compatibility, sympa-

thy, admiration, familiarity and

many other shades of emotion.

—*Alexandra Kollontai*

18

19

Vanessa Bell. *Tile design: Autumn,* c. 1950. Oil and gouache on paper, 27½ x 27½ in.
Anthony d'Offay Gallery, London.

Individual personal freedom,
culminating in perfected sexual liberty, is indeed a pearl
of great price, whose value is
beyond computation.

—*Victoria Woodhull*
in Elixir of Life *speech*

20

21

But what connection is there
between the pertness of coquetry
and the sentiment of love? It is very
possible, too, that men may be very
much interested, very much amused,
particularly by the attachment which
beauty inspires, by the hope or the
certainty of captivating it; but what
connection has this kind of impres-
sion with the sentiment of love?

—*Germaine de Staël*
in Influence of Passion

22

23

24

25

In love and in submission we are
given the gift of ourselves, we are
made more actual, more encompass-
ing, more wedded to ourselves, and
this alone is the true efficacy of love,
giving life and joy.

—Lou Andreas-Salomé
in The Freud Journal

26

27

28

Sensuality, wanting a
religion, invented love.

—Natalie Barney

29

30

For marriages built upon the shifting

sands of fear, shame and ignorance

can never lead to happiness, yet if

contracted with a frank recognition

of the central importance of the

beauty of sex in life, alike in its phys-

iological, psychological and spiritual

aspects, happiness becomes a glow-

ing possibility. This is a buried trea-

sure to be unearthed by true lovers.

—*Margaret Sanger*
in Happiness in Marriage

31

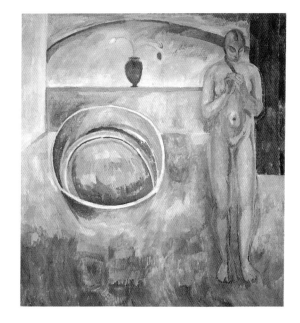

Vanessa Bell. *The Tub*. Tate Gallery, London/Art Resource, New York.

September

Simone de Beauvoir

FRENCH, 1908–1986

Simone de Beauvoir was made famous by the publication of her feminist manifesto *Le Deuxième Sexe* [The Second Sex] (1949), which examined the causes of women's oppression. She shared her life with existentialist Jean-Paul Sartre, whom she met when they were both students of philosophy at the Sorbonne, but the two never married. Simone believed that fidelity inhibited self-discovery and therefore accepted Sartre's many affairs and had a few of her own. Her first fictional novel, *She Came to Stay* (1949), was based on a love triangle involving Sartre, herself and a young student named Olga. In *The Mandarins* (1956) Simone used fictional characters to recount her love affair with American writer Nelson Algren. She also published a four-volume autobiographical series that chronicled her life from childhood through adulthood, including intimate moments from her relationship with Sartre.

1

2

Feminine sexual excitement can
reach an intensity unknown to man.
Male sex excitement is keen but
localized and it leaves the man quite
in possession of himself; woman, on
the contrary, really loses her mind.

—Simone de Beauvoir
in The Second Sex

3

4

5

To have a radical understand-
ing with someone is, in any
case, a great privilege. In my
eyes it is literally priceless.

—Simone de Beauvoir
in The Prime of Life

6

7

Theda Bara

AMERICAN, 1890–1955

Theda Bara was the first seductress of silent film. Legend contended that she was the offspring of a sheikh and a princess; in reality, however, she was just Theodosia Goodman from Cincinnati, Ohio. Theda Bara became famous overnight, and brought great success to director William Fox, for her performance in the film *A Fool There Was* (1915). The screen role of "vamp" was born and immediately catapulted her into stardom. Theda appeared in over thirty films in the course of her career. Their titles—*Tiger Woman, The She Devil, The Vixen and Sin, Salomé, Cleopatra, Carmen, Romeo and Juliet* and *The Darling of Paris,* among others—are indicative of her screen personality.

8

9

Being a feminist, convinced that a woman's private life should be economically sound before she should indulge in her own romantic impulses, I saw a public that would support me.

—*Theda Bara*
in "How I Became a Film Vampire,"
Forum, *June/July 1919*

10

11

12

An actress should be a plastic human being, a woman who surrenders herself to her imagination, without moral analysis.

—*Theda Bara*
in "How I Became a
Film Vampire," Forum,
June/July 1919

13

14

15

I here throw down my gauntlet, and
deny the existence of sexual virtues,
not excepting modesty. For man
and woman, truth, if I understand
the meaning of the word, must be
the same.

—*Mary Wollstonecraft*
in The Vindication of
the Rights of Woman

16

17

18

When the heart and reason
accord there is no flying
from voluptuous sensations, I
find, do what a woman can.

—*Mary Wollstonecraft*

19

Mary Wollstonecraft

ENGLISH, 1759–1797

In 1792 Mary Wollstonecraft shocked London with the publication of her book *The Vindication of the Rights of Woman,* which advocated women's freedom and equality between the sexes. Mary argued that women were held back by their lack of access to education, and she denounced the institution of marriage as oppressive to women. She highlighted the struggle between erotic passion and the power of reason and preached moderation of erotic passion in marriage. Mary was ostracized for her unconventional life-style, her many passionate affairs, her bearing of a child out of wedlock and her economic independence. She died at age thirty-seven shortly after giving birth to her second daughter, Mary, who would write *Frankenstein.*

20

21

Louise Brooks

AMERICAN, 1906–1985

Silent film actor Louise Brooks personified eros on the screen. Born in Kansas, she began her career as a dancer and later turned to acting in such Hollywood films as *The American Venus, Love 'em and Leave 'em* and *A Girl in Every Port*. She became the embodiment of "amoral" sexuality in her role as Lulu in the German film *Pandora's Box* (1929), directed by G. W. Pabst. Based on Frank Wedekind's play, in *Pandora's Box* Lulu unwittingly seduces an upper-class German man, becomes the victim of prostitution and is murdered by Jack the Ripper. Louise is also famous for her role in Pabst's *Diary of a Lost Girl*, the story of a young woman who is seduced and becomes pregnant at age sixteen, is sent to a sadistically run reformatory and ends up in a brothel. Both films met with censorship for their sexual explicitness and hostile audience reaction. After returning to America at age twenty-four, Louise played a few bit parts in Hollywood films and continued to dance, but she became increasingly isolated. Her memoirs were published under the title of *Lulu in Hollywood.*

22

23

Love is a publicity stunt, and making love—after the first curious raptures—is only another petulant way to pass the time waiting for the studio to call.

—*Louise Brooks*
in a letter to James Card,
December 17, 1955

24

25

There can be no doubt about it, sex is basic to security. If you think you fail in that, nothing else can compensate for this inner sense of humiliation. Thank God, at thirty-five I banished my shame and Puritan background and learned how to please others and myself.

—*Louise Brooks*
in a letter to Kevin Brownlow,
August 25, 1966

26

27

28

In effect, what is the liberty that a woman can seize? . . . adultery.

—George Sand
in a speech before members
of the Central Committee
of the Left

29

30

IV

I shall forget you presently, my dear,
So make the most of this, your little day,
Your little month, your little half year,
Ere I forget, or die, or move away,
And we are done forever; by and by
I shall forget you, as I said, but now,
If you entreat me with your loveliest lie
I will protest you with my favorite vow.
I would indeed that love were longer-lived,
And vows were not so brittle as they are,
But so it is, and nature has contrived
To struggle on without a break thus far,—
Whether or not we find what we are seeking
Is idle, biologically speaking.

—Edna St. Vincent Millay
in A Few Figs from Thistles

I make the claim boldly that from the very moment woman is emancipated from the necessity of yielding the control of her sexual organs to man to insure a home, food and clothing, the doom of sexual demoralization will be sealed. From that moment there will be no sexual intercourse except such as is desired by women.

—Victoria Woodhull
in Tried as by Fire

October

Marie Laurencin

FRENCH, 1885–1956

Marie Laurencin has been associated with the cubists through her friendships with Picasso and Braque, yet her style remained artistically independent and distinctly feminine. She was one of the few women painters in twentieth-century Paris who refused to emulate the male-dominated art world. Throughout her life she painted pastel portraits of women—primitive figures in dreamlike states and many self-portraits. Despite her five-year romance with poet Guillaume Apollinaire and her subsequent marriage and divorce, she found solace primarily in the company of women, which is reflected in her exclusive portrayal of the female figure.

1.

2

If I feel so distant from other painters, it is because they are men—and men appear to me like problems that are difficult to resolve. …But if the genius of man intimidates me, I feel perfectly at ease with everything that is feminine.

—*Marie Laurencin*

3

4

The censure "with a difference" extended by our gracious world to male and female offenders—the crushing into dust for the woman—and the "oh you naughty man" ism for the betrayer—appears to me an injustice which cries upwards from the earth.

—*Elizabeth Barrett Browning*

Marie Laurencin. *Femme à la Colombe* [Woman with Dove], 1919. Oil, 60 x 50 cm. Musée National d'Art Moderne. Centre Georges Pompidou, Paris.

5

6

In the marriage relation it is
supremely true that only by
loosening the bonds can one
bind two hearts indissolubly
together.

—Marie Stopes
in Married Love

7

8

9

10

11

The passion of love is our deepest
entry into ourself, it is a thousandfold
solitude.... The loved object is... only
the cause that gives rise to this.

—*Lou Andreas-Salomé*

12

13

14

When motherhood becomes the fruit of a deep yearning, not the result of ignorance or accident, its children will become the foundation of a new race.

—*Margaret Sanger*
in Woman and the New Race

15

Your desire, sole master of your bed, remains the nocturnal creator of your joy.

—*Natalie Barney*

16

17

Marie Laurencin. *La Repetition* [The Rehearsal], 1938 . Oil, 120 x 120 cm. Musée National d'Art Moderne. Centre Georges Pompidou, Paris.

18

But the intuition of those who stand
midway between the two sexes is so
ruthless, so poignant, so accurate, so
deadly as to be in the nature of an
added scourge.

—*Radclyffe Hall*
in The Well of Loneliness

19

Marie Laurencin. *Nu* [Nude]. Oil on canvas, 10⅜ x 16¼ in. Museum of Fine Arts, Springfield,
Massachusetts. Gift of Mrs. Howard K. Bemis in memory of Howard Kenyon Bemis.

20

He was my cream, and I was
his coffee...and when you
poured us together, it was
something.

—*Josephine Baker*
describing her affair with
the crown prince of Sweden

21

22

So, unhesitatingly, without fear or
reserve, at some moment of culmina-
tion when all separation is over,
except that delight of separation—
which is consciousness of mixing—
bodies unite; the human love has its
gratification.

—*Virginia Woolf*
in A Room of One's Own

23

24

25

26

> In the limitless desert of love, sensual pleasure has an ardent but very small place, so incandescent that at first one sees nothing else.
>
> —*Colette*

27

28

> Free love? As if love is anything but free!...Man has conquered whole nations, but all his armies could not conquer love. Man has chained and fettered the spirit, but he has been utterly helpless before love....Yes, love is free; it can dwell in no other atmosphere.
>
> —*Emma Goldman*
> *in* Marriage and Love

29

Any one she is kissing is one she is
kissing then, not kissing again and
again, not kissing and kissing, any
one she is kissing is one she kissed
then, is one she did kiss then, one
she kissed some then.

— *Gertrude Stein*
in Many Many Women

30

31

Marie Laurencin. *Leda and the Swan*, 1923. Oil on canvas, 26½ x 32 in. Philadelphia
Museum of Art. Gift of Mr. and Mrs. Charles C. G. Chaplin.

November

Isadora Duncan

AMERICAN, 1878–1927

Isadora Duncan pioneered modern dance. From an early age she rejected classical ballet and improvised her own radical dance movements, which she performed barefoot. Her performances received mediocre reviews in the U.S. but were raved about in Europe..

Isadora believed in the free expression of her body and accordingly wore loose-fitting classical tunics and sandals. She also strongly endorsed free love. She had many relationships, most notably with stage designer Gordon Craig, millionaire Paris Singer and Russian poet Sergei Yesenin, whom she married in 1922. The couple divorced a year later. Isadora died in 1927 following an accident in which her scarf got caught in the wheel of her car.

1

Any intelligent woman who
reads the marriage contract,
and then, goes into it,
deserves all the consequences.

—*Isadora Duncan*
in My Life

2

3

4

Now that I had discovered that Love
might be a pastime as well as a
tragedy, I gave myself to it with
pagan innocence. Men seem to be
hungry for Beauty, hungry for that
love which refreshes and inspires
without fear or responsibility.

—*Isadora Duncan*
in My Life

5

6

7

In a word, women are bound
by the sympathies of the
heart; but with men these
ties are not so sacred.

—*Germaine de Staël*
in Influence of Passion

8

9

In whatever situation we may be

placed by a deep-rooted passion, I

can never believe that it misleads us

from the path of virtue. Every thing

is sacrifice, every thing is indiffer-

ence to our own gratifications in the

exalted attachment of love; selfish-

ness alone degrades. Every thing is

goodness, every thing is pity in the

10

heart that truly loves. Inhumanity

alone banishes all morality from the

heart of man.

—*Germaine de Staël*
in Influence of Passion

11

Germaine de Staël

FRENCH, 1766–1817

Germaine de Staël was a pioneer of French romanticism and the head of a salon that became a powerful intellectual and political center in Paris. In her striving to find the "perfect love," her love life was always complicated and unconventional. Germaine felt that nothing in life held equal value to being loved and that life without love was spiritual death. Her dissatisfaction with her marriage to Baron Staël-Holstein, a Swedish diplomat, led to many affairs, including a five-year liaison with a man with whom she had children. Yet none of the affairs provided her with the intensity of love and passion she desired. Among Germaine's writings were two very popular novels, *Delphine* (1803) and *Corinne* (1807), which contained self-portraits on the theme of a woman's right to free love.

12

13

Portrait by François Gérard. Engraved by E. Scriven. Courtesy Library of Congress.

Aphra Behn

ENGLISH, 1640–1689

Aphra Behn was the first woman known to earn her living as a professional writer and to write as candidly about sexuality as men. She believed that love should be free and not forced by parents or controlled by social conventions and that men and women should love freely and equally. Her first three plays, *The Forced Marriage, The Amorous Prince* and *The Dutch Lover,* all statements against arranged marriage, played successfully in London. Her most popular play, *The Rover,* had as its theme the idea that marriage for money was a form of prostitution. When the popularity of the stage waned, Aphra turned her attention to writing poetry and novels. Her readers were shocked by *The Disappointment,* erotic verse about female sexual desire and male impotence, and by her portrayal of lesbianism in *To the Fair Clarinda.* Her most famous novel, *Oroonko,* was a passionate protest against slavery.

14

15

16

All the desires of mutual love

are virtuous.

—*Aphra Behn*

17

THE WILLING MISTRESS

Amyntas led me to a Grove,
 Where all the Trees did shade us;
The Sun it self, though it had Strove,
 It could not have betray'd us.
The Place secur'd from humane eyes
 No other fear allows
But when the Winds that gently rise
 Doe Kiss the yielding Boughs.

Down there we satt upon the Moss,
 And did begin to play
A Thousand Amorous Tricks, to pass
 The heat of all the day.
A many Kisses he did give:
 And I return'd the same
Which made me willing to receive
 That which I dare not name.

His Charming Eyes no Aid requir'd
 To tell their softning Tale:
On her that was already fir'd,
 'Twas easy to prevaile.
He did but Kiss and Clasp me round,
 Whilst those his thoughts Exprest:
And lay'd me gently on the Ground;
 Ah who can guess the rest?

—*Aphra Behn in a song from* The Dutch Lover

Who can be happy without love? For
me, I never numbered those dull
days amongst those of my life, in
which I had not my soul filled with
that soft passion.

    —*Aphra Behn*

Alexandra Kollontai

RUSSIAN, 1872–1952

Alexandra Kollontai was the first
woman to serve on the Central
Committee of Lenin's party. She was
an avid campaigner for sexual equality and spoke out against domestic-
ity and the inequalities in marriage;
alternatively she advocated free love
and collective living. Her outspoken
views on the "woman question" were
criticized by party members, and
eventually Stalin had her banished
to a life of diplomatic posts.

Kollontai held as an ideal a relationship in which a woman could
satisfy her desire for intimacy without sacrificing her independence or
work. She wrote about this theme in
Lover of Worker Bees (1923) and
*The Autobiography of a Sexually
Emancipated Woman* (1926).

18

19

20

21

Love, in and of itself, is a great, creative force; it broadens and enriches
the psyche of him who feels it and
him on whom it is bestowed. There
is no doubt that love will become the
cult of future humanity.

—Alexandra Kollontai

22

23

The normal woman seeks in sexual
intercourse completeness and har-
mony; the man, reared on prostitution, overlooking the complex
vibrations of love's sensations, fol-
lows only his pallid, monotone, physical inclinations, leaving sensations
of incompleteness and spiritual
hunger on both sides.

—Alexandra Kollontai

24

25

26

27

I love and dance with my
dream unfurled, trusting
darkness, trusting the
labyrinth, into the furnaces
of love.

—*Anaïs Nin*
in Cities of the Interiors

28

29

30

December

Anaïs Nin

AMERICAN, BORN FRANCE, 1903–1977

Anaïs Nin was noted for her poetic fiction and her literary explorations of the female psyche and sexuality. An early patient of Jung, she brought to her writing a deep interest in the unconscious. Among others, her novels include *The House of Incest* (1936), an exploration of incest as a form of self-love; *Winter of Artifice* (1939), a psychological analysis of a father-daughter relationship; *This Hunger* (1945), a collection of stories about women who are afraid of people, especially men; *Ladders to Fire* (1946), stories of women in search of identity; and *A Spy in the House of Love* (1954), a woman's self-examination of her many transient love relationships. Encouraged by her friend Henry Miller, Nin also wrote two volumes of erotica: *Delta of Venus* and *Little Birds.* Published portions of her ten-volume diary have been acclaimed by feminists as a model for sexual and emotional liberation.

1

2

3

4

In the feverish caresses and love-
making that bound me to the man of
my choice I could discern the movements of my heart, my freedom as an
individual. But that mood of solitary,
languorous excitement cried out for
anyone, regardless.

—Simone de Beauvoir
in The Prime of Life

5

6

Women deceive themselves,
too, quite as much as they
deceive others; for in imagination they defy all conventions.

—Theda Bara
in "How I Became
a Film Vampire," Forum,
June/July 1919

7

Suzanne Valadon

FRENCH, 1865–1938

Suzanne Valadon painted during the impressionist period and was most noted for her sensuous nudes. Initially an artists' model, she soon discovered her own talent and was encouraged by Toulouse-Lautrec and received instruction from Degas.

Suzanne bore a son to one of her many lovers but never revealed the father's identity. Her most productive years as a painter began at age forty-four, when she met and fell in love with her son's friend Andre Utter, twenty-one years her junior. During the next five years she painted her most famous nudes, including *Adam and Eve*, a depiction of herself and Utter in the Garden of Eden, and *Casting the Nets*, one of the first paintings in the modern era by a woman of a male nude.

8

9

10

11

12

You have to be hard on yourself, be
honest, and look yourself in the face.
You have to get rid of the surplus,
the hatred and the excessive love.

—*Suzanne Valadon*

Suzanne Valadon. *La Chambre Bleue* [The Blue Room], 1923. Oil on canvas, 35⁷⁄₁₆ x 45¼ in.
Musée National d'Art Moderne. Centre Georges Pompidou, Paris.

The great art of films does
not consist in descriptive
movement of face and body,
but in the movements of
thought and soul transmitted
in a kind of intense isolation.

—*Louise Brooks*

13

14

Love, from its very nature, must be
transitory. To seek for a secret that
would render it consistent, would
be as wild a search as for the
philosopher's stone, or the grand
panacea; and the discovery would
be equally useless, or rather perni-
cious, to mankind.

—Mary Wollstonecraft
in The Vindication of
the Rights of Woman

15

16

17

18

19

> I have never been loved with a passion approaching my own.
>
> —*Germaine de Staël*

20

21

> The dancer of the future will be one whose body and soul have grown so harmoniously together that the natural language of that soul will have become the movement of the body.... O, She is coming, the dancer of the future: the free spirit who will inhabit the body of new woman...the highest intelligence in the freest body!
>
> —*Isadora Duncan*

22

But when the wave of passion
sweeps over her, she does not
renounce the brilliant smile of life,
she does not hypocritically wrap herself up in a faded cloak of female
virtue. No, she holds out her hand to
her chosen one ... to drink from the
cup of love's joy, however deep it is,
and to satisfy herself. When the cup
is empty, she throws it away without
regret and bitterness.

—*Alexandra Kollontai*

23

24

25

In the struggle of man to gain command over his body, and in the slow and often back sliding evolution of the higher love, there is no doubt that humanity owes much to the ascetic. But this debt is in the past.

—*Marie Stopes*
in Married Love

26

Suzanne Valadon. *Négresse Nue* [Nude Negress]. Musées de Menton France.

To what does modern marriage amount, if it be not to hold sexual slaves, who otherwise would be free?

—*Victoria Woodhull*
in Elixir of Life *speech*

27

28

Sex expression, rightly understood, is the consummation of love, its completion and its consecration.

—*Margaret Sanger*
in Happiness in Marriage

29

30

31